Let's Play

PIANO

A complete course for young beginners

PART ONE

First published in the U.K. in 2017 by
The Ashton Book Company
9 Dairy Farm, Ashton Keynes,
Swindon, Wiltshire SN6 6NZ
All rights reserved

ISBN-13: 978-1548024024
ISBN-10: 1548024023

FOREWORD

This course has been designed for young beginners who are taking their first piano lessons. The basics of piano playing and music reading are presented step by step and there are lots of tunes to play so that each new skill can be thoroughly practiced.

WELL KNOWN TUNES
As much as possible, well know tunes are used, in very easy arrangements, so that students know what they should sound like when they are playing on their own.

ACCOMPANIMENTS
Many of the tunes have accompaniments which can be played by a teacher or parent in order to make a more satisfying performance and to encourage the students to play rhythmically.

QUICK QUIZ PAGES
These pages give the student the opportunity to revise what they have learnt by doing a fun and easy quiz.

WISE OWL HELPS OUT
The yellow owl appears regularly in order to explain important points and new information.

CONTENTS

INTRODUCTION 4
    Musical Notation
    Note Lengths
    Note Names
    Finger Numbers
    How to Hold Your Hands on the Keys

LET'S PLAY C - WITH THE RIGHT HAND 6
    Four Time March
    Now I See

LET'S PLAY C - WITH THE LEFT HAND 7
    On the March Again

USING BOTH HANDS 7
    Right, Left, Quick march

LET'S PLAY D 8
    Direct Current

LET'S PLAY B 8
    Bee in the Garden

TWO TOGETHER 9
    2 Plus 2 Makes Great!

QUICK QUIZ 10

LET'S PLAY E 11
    Up to E and Back Again
    Merrily We Roll Along
    I Saw a Unicorn

LET'S PLAY A 13
    Sad Song

QUICK QUIZ 11

REPEAT DOTS 15
    Deep Blue Horizon

LET'S PLAY LEFT HAND G 16
    Hot Cross Buns
    Au Clair de la Lune
    Twinkle, Twinkle Little Star
    Frere Jacques

LET'S PLAY RIGHT HAND F 18
    Take It Easy
    Yankee Doodle

Shopping Trolley

LET'S PLAY RIGHT HAND G 20

Lightly Row

LET'S PLAY LEFT HAND F 21

In the Forest

This is Not a Tune

RESTS 22

Take a Rest

Feel the Beat

A NEW TIME SIGNATURE 23

Half a Pound of Tupenny Rice

THE DOTTED MINIM 24

I Saw a Ghost

THE QUAVER 25

Lavender's Blue

We Three Kings

QUICK QUIZ 27

THE UPBEAT 28

For He's a Jolly Good Fellow

THE TIE 30

All Tied Up

My Hat it has Three Corners

Happy Birthday to You

PLAYING HANDS TOGETHER 32

Hands together - Fingers 12345

Hands together - Take It Slow

Kum Ba Yah

MUSICAL TERMS: TEMPO 33

Hurry, Hurry

Trotting Along

Together Again

AMAZING GRACE 34

QUICK QUIZ 34

MUSICAL TERMS: DYNAMICS 35

The Tortoise

The Sprinter

The Mocking Bird

OLD MACDONALD HAD A FARM 36

STACCATO 37

Fruit and Nuts

The Clock

Some Folks Do

FINGER GYM 38

Digital Keep Fit

Technical Tips

WHEN THE SAINTS GO MARCHING IN 39

INTRODUCTION

MUSICAL NOTATION

Music is written on a set of 5 lines called a stave.
The right hand stave has a treble clef and the left hand stave has a bass clef.

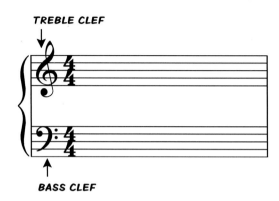

Music is divided into bars, with a line at the end of each one. These lines are called bar lines.

The numbers after the clef sign are called the time signature. They tell us how many beats there are in each bar.

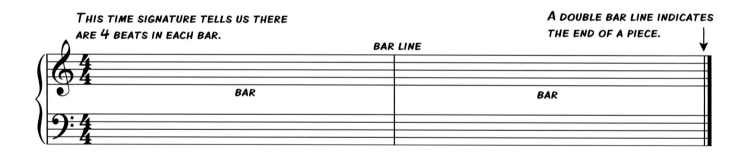

Notes are written on the staves and their position tells you which note to play on the piano. Notes that are higher on the stave are played further to the right of the keyboard and they sound higher. For example, each note here is higher than the one before:

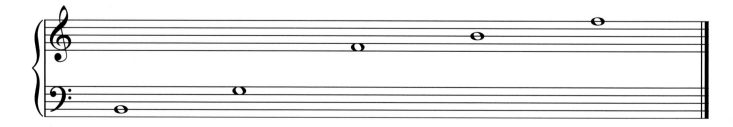

NOTE LENGTHS

Music has a beat and the way notes are written shows how many beats they should be held for:

𝗈 = 4 beats - this is called a semibreve or a whole note

♩ = 2 beats - this is called a minim or a half note

♩ = 1 beat - this is called a crotchet or a quarter note

NOTE NAMES

Each note on the piano has a letter name. There are only 7 letters used - A B C D E F and G.

FINGER NUMBERS

Your fingers are numbered 1 to 5 in each hand. When you read piano music you will notice that many notes have a number above or below them telling you which finger to use.

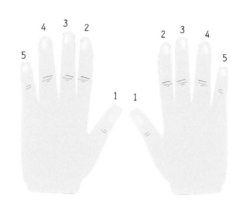

HOW TO HOLD YOUR HANDS ON THE KEYS

When you play you should hold your hands in a relaxed shape with fingers gently curved so that the tips touch the keys.

LET'S PLAY C – WITH THE RIGHT HAND

The first note we will learn to play is middle C
with the right hand.

If you look at the piano keys, middle C is the C that
is nearest to the middle of the keyboard.

It looks like this in the music. Notice, it is not on any of the 5 lines that make
up the stave but has a small line of it's own just underneath the stave.

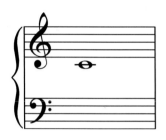

Remember

C is to the left of
two black keys!

Here are your first two tunes, both using middle C. You will be playing middle C with your thumb.
Count as you play and remember to hold each note for the correct number of beats.

FOUR TIME MARCH

*THE NUMBER 1 ABOVE THE NOTE TELLS
YOU TO PLAY THIS NOTE WITH YOUR THUMB.*

NOW I SEE

LET'S PLAY C – WITH THE LEFT HAND

When middle C is to be played with the left hand it is written on the bass clef stave. It looks like this in the music:

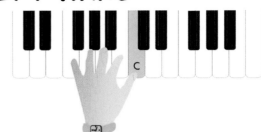

Play the next tune with your left hand thumb.

ON THE MARCH AGAIN!

USING BOTH HANDS

The next tune uses both hands When the notes are in the bass clef, use the left hand. When the notes are in the treble clef, use the right hand.

RIGHT, LEFT, QUICK MARCH

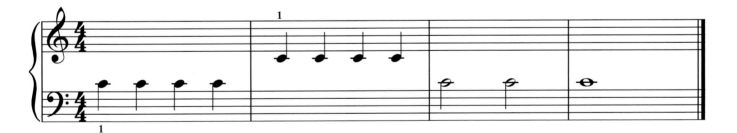

Accompaniment for LEFT, RIGHT, QUICK MARCH

LET'S PLAY D

D is next to C and you should play it with finger 2 of your right hand.

SAY THESE NOTE NAMES

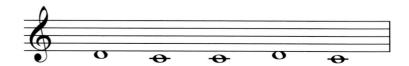

DIRECT CURRENT

LET'S PLAY B

B is on the left of C and you should play it with finger 2 of your left hand.

Bee sits on the top of the 5 lines

BEE IN THE GARDEN

TWO TOGETHER!

The next tune uses C and D in the right hand plus C and B
in the left hand, thats 2 plus 2!
It's another duet. You can play it on your own but it will
sound much better if you ask your teacher to play
the accompaniment with you.

2 PLUS 2 MAKES GREAT!

Accompaniment for 2 PLUS 2 MAKES GREAT!

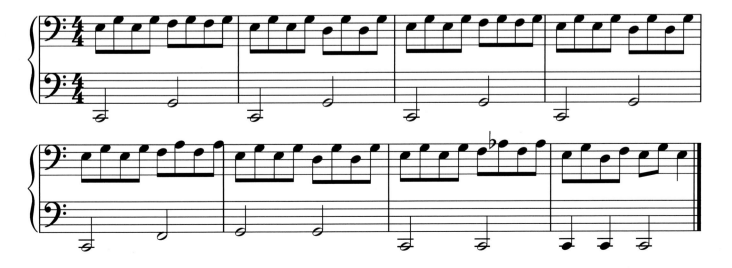

QUICK QUIZ

You have learnt a lot so far but how well can you remember it all?
Try this quiz to test youself.

MARKS

1. Underneath each note write how many beats it should last:

/10

2. Name these notes (ie write the letter name):

/5

/5

3. Give the name of these symbols:

 _____   𝄢 _____

/2

4. Draw each of these notes:

a crotchet (quarter note)

/3

a semibreve (whole note)

a minim (half note)

Total Marks   /25

LET'S PLAY E

Play E with finger 3 of your right hand.

UP TO E AND BACK AGAIN

MERRILY WE ROLL ALONG

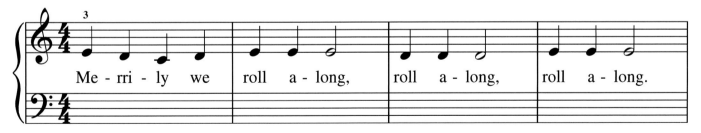

Me - rri - ly we | roll a - long, | roll a - long, | roll a - long.

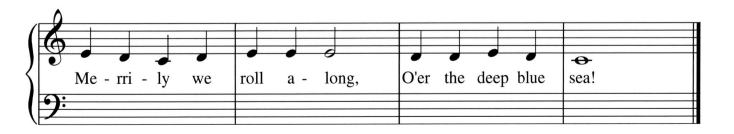

Me - rri - ly we | roll a - long, | O'er the deep blue | sea!

The next tune moves between your right hand and your left hand. As it moves from one hand to the next try to keep it flowing in time.

SAY THESE NOTE NAMES

I SAW A UNICORN

Accompaniment for I SAW A UNICORN

Let's Play A

Play A with finger 3 of your left hand.

Remember ALWAYS FOLLOW THE FINGERING AS WELL AS THE NOTES

When you play "Sad Song" try to make it sound sad by playing fairly quietly and not too quickly

SAD SONG

QUICK QUIZ

1. Name these notes:

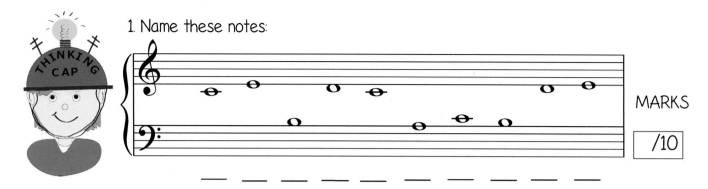

MARKS

/10

2. Write the correct finger numbers above these notes:

/10

3. Draw these notes in the treble clef:

a crotchet E   a minim C   a semibreve D   a minim E   a crotchet D

/10

4. Draw these notes in the bass clef:

a crotchet C   a semibreve B   a minim A   a crotchet B   a minim C

/10

5. Complete these musical sums (the first one has been done for you):

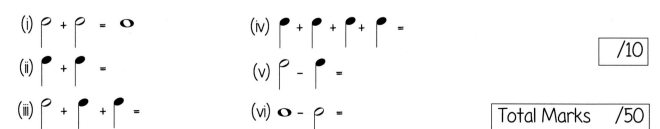

/10

Total Marks   /50

REPEAT DOTS

If you see two dots just next to a double bar line it means that you should repeat the music from the beginning.

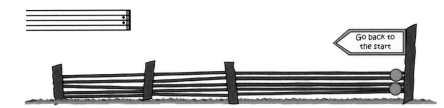

DEEP BLUE HORIZON

Accompaniment for DEEP BLUE HORIZON

LET'S PLAY LEFT HAND G

Play G with finger 4 of your left hand.

4

HOT CROSS BUNS

2   3   4

Find your pencil

Write in the note names

AU CLAIR DE LA LUNE

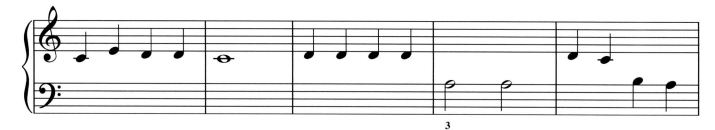

3

TWINKLE, TWINKLE LITTLE STAR

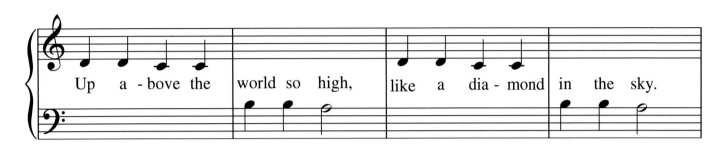

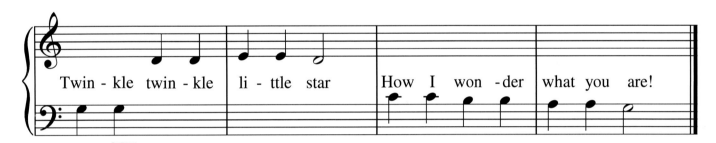

FRERE JACQUES

LET'S PLAY RIGHT HAND F

Play F with finger 4 of your right hand.

TAKE IT EASY

Take it ea -sy take it slow, here's a -no -ther note you know.

Find your pencil

Write in the note names

TIME SIGNATURES

As you know, the time signature 4/4 means 4 beats in each bar. It is sometimes abbreviated to **C** which is short for "common time".

YANKEE DOODLE

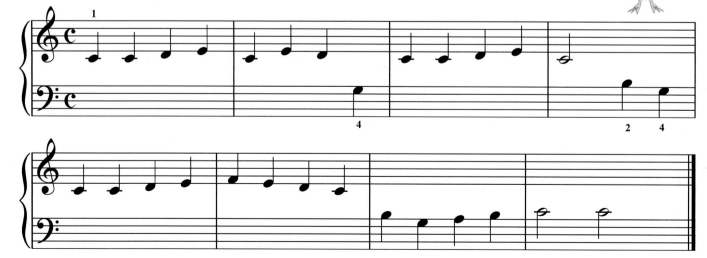

SHOPPING TROLLEY

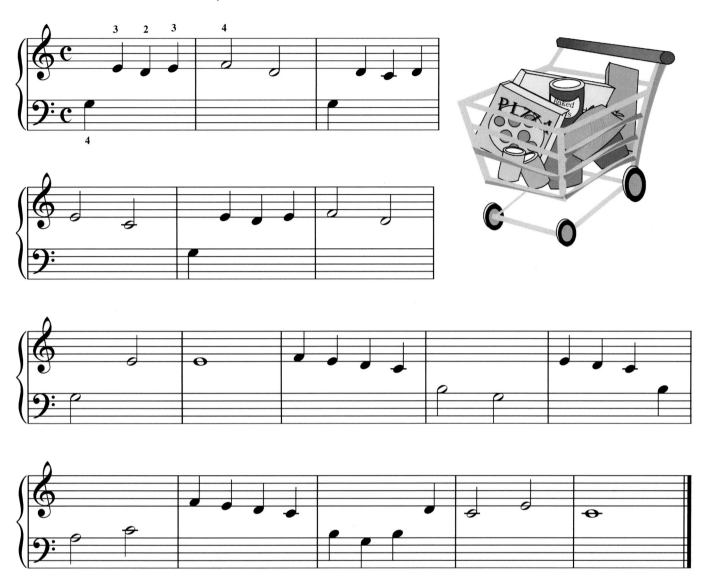

Accompaniment for SHOPPING TROLLEY

LET'S PLAY RIGHT HAND G

Play G with finger 5 of your right hand.

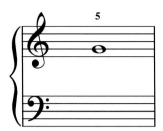

I JUST WANT TO RIDE MY BIKE

Find your pencil

Well done, you have now learnt 5 notes in the right hand!
They are C, D, E, F and G. But can you name them?
Here are the 5 notes you have learnt - write the name under each one
(the first 2 have been done for you).

E   F   __ __ __ __ __ __ __ __ __ __

Here is a tune which uses all of the right hand notes you now know

LIGHTLY ROW

Light - ly row,   light - ly row,   O'er the glass- y   waves we go!

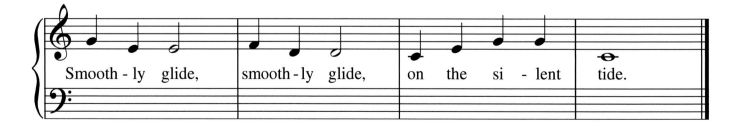

Smooth - ly glide,   smooth - ly glide,   on the si - lent   tide.

LET'S PLAY LEFT HAND F

Play F with finger 5 of your left hand.

IN THE FOREST

In the for -est far a - way, I saw an owl!

You now know 5 left hand notes

F   G   A   B   C

Find your pencil

To help you to remember which note is which you should practise writing them here. (The first 2 have been done for you)

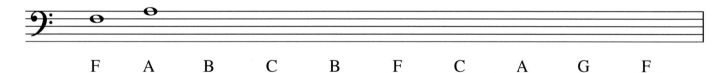

F   A   B   C   B   F   C   A   G   F

THIS IS NOT A TUNE

You should try to memorize all 5 of the left hand notes you have learnt so far. Here they all are, jumbled up! Try to play through these as fast as you can. They do not make any sort of tune though.

22

RESTS

You already know these note values:

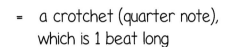 = a semibreve (whole note), which is 4 beats long

♩ = a minim (half note), which is 2 beats long

♩ = a crotchet (quarter note),
which is 1 beat long

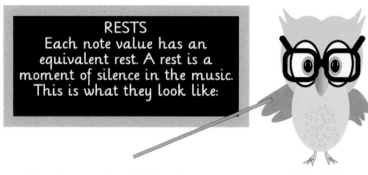

RESTS
Each note value has an
equivalent rest. A rest is a
moment of silence in the music.
This is what they look like:

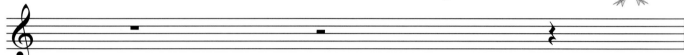

this is a semibreve rest
which is 4 beats long

this is a minim rest
which is 2 beats long

this is a crotchet rest
which is 1 beat long

Here are two tunes which will give you practice at counting rests. Try to count as you play so that you can make sure you rest for the correct amount of time.

TAKE A REST

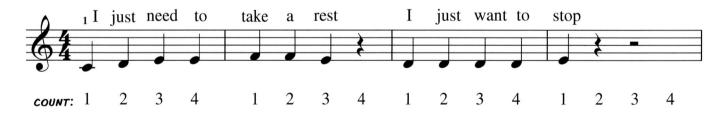

I just need to take a rest   I just want to stop

COUNT: 1 2 3 4   1 2 3 4   1 2 3 4   1 2 3 4

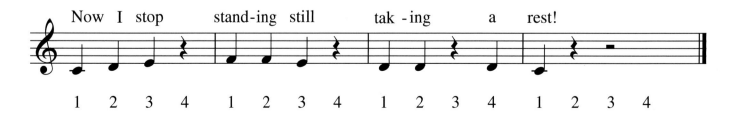

Now I stop stand-ing still tak-ing a rest!

1 2 3 4   1 2 3 4   1 2 3 4   1 2 3 4

FEEL THE BEAT

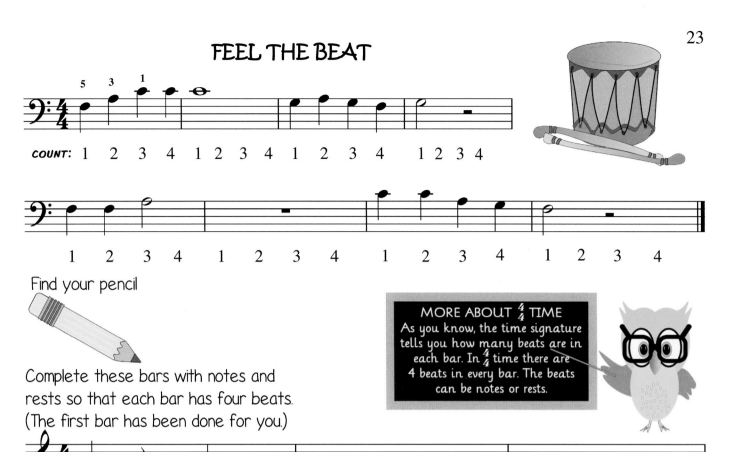

Find your pencil

Complete these bars with notes and rests so that each bar has four beats. (The first bar has been done for you.)

MORE ABOUT 4/4 TIME
As you know, the time signature tells you how many beats are in each bar. In 4/4 time there are 4 beats in every bar. The beats can be notes or rests.

A NEW TIME SIGNATURE

The 3/4 time signature is used to show that each bar has only 3 beats.

Tunes with the 3/4 time signature are said to be in 3 time (or triple time) and tunes with the 4/4 time signature are said to be in 4 time (or quadruple time).

HALF A POUND OF TUPENNY RICE

THE DOTTED MINIM

A dotted minim (or dotted half note) looks just like a minim but has a small dot to the right of the note head:

It is held for 3 beats.

I SAW A GHOST!

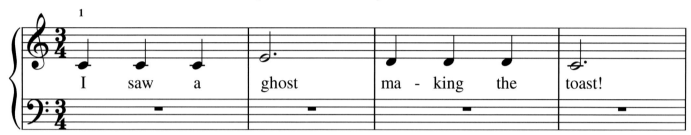

I saw a ghost ma - king the toast!

I saw an elf right on the shelf!

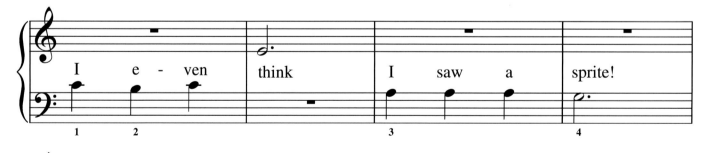

I e - ven think I saw a sprite!

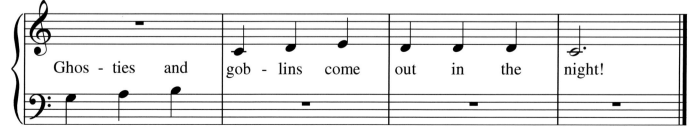

Ghos - ties and gob - lins come out in the night!

THE QUAVER

A quaver (or eighth note) looks a bit like a crotchet, but there is a
little tail on the end of the stem:

A quaver lasts for half of a beat.
Quavers often appear in pairs with the tails joined together like this:

A quaver rest looks like this:

Quavers are
QUICKER!

CLAPPING GAME

Ask your teacher to clap this rhythm, then you copy it

LAVENDER'S BLUE

La ven - der's | blue dill -y dill -y | La ven der's | green.

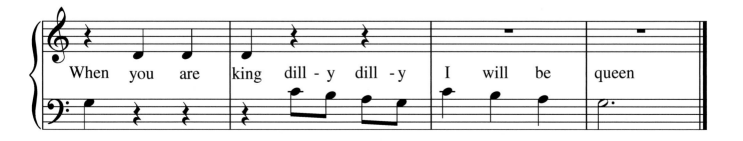

When you are | king dill - y dill -y | I will be | queen

THE PAUSE SIGN

If you see this sign above a
note it means that you should
hold that note for a little
longer – ie. pause on the note.

WE THREE KINGS OF ORIENT ARE

It may not be Christmas, but this tune is a nice one for any time of year!

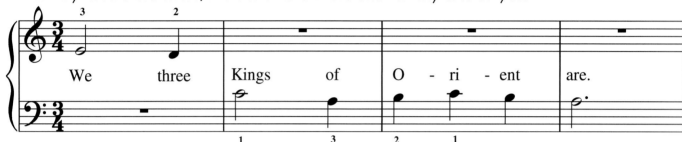

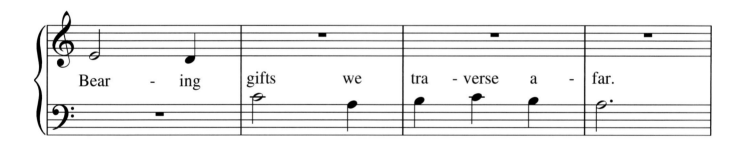

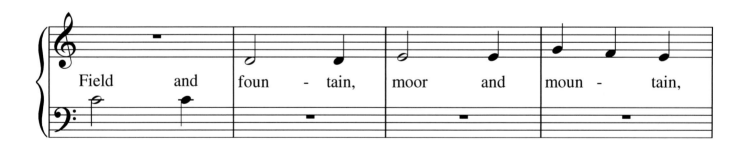

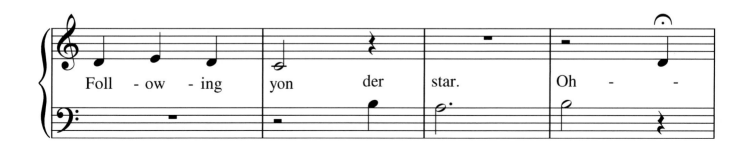

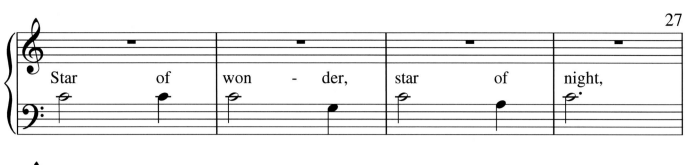

Star of won - der, star of night,

Star with ro - yal beau - ty bright.

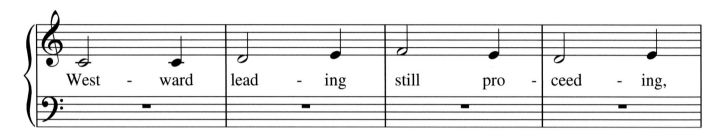

West - ward lead - ing still pro - ceed - ing,

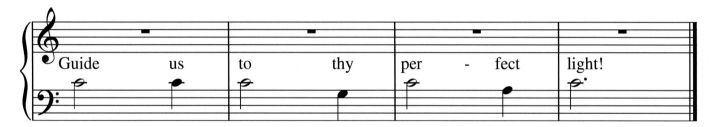

Guide us to thy per - fect light!

QUICK QUIZ

1. Draw these notes:

a crotchet D   a minim E   a dotted minim F   a semibreve G

MARKS

/4

2. Draw these rests:

a crotchet   a minim   a semibreve

/3

3. How many beats are in each of these notes:

a crotchet (quarter note) =

a minim (half note) =

a semibreve (whole note) =

a dotted minim (dotted half note) =

/8

Total marks   /15

THE UPBEAT

THE UPBEAT
Sometimes the first bar of a tune has fewer beats than the others. This happens when the tune starts on an upbeat.
If a tune starts with an upbeat, the number of beats in the final bar is usually adjusted so that, when added together, the beats in the first and last bar add up to one whole bar.

In the following tune, the first bar has one beat and the last bar has two beats, so between the two bars there are three beats.

FOR HE'S A JOLLY GOOD FELLOW

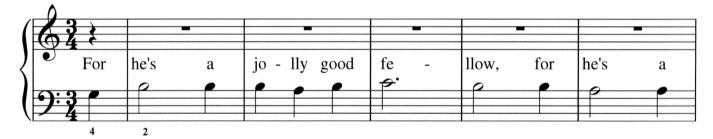

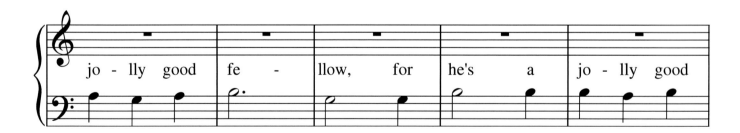

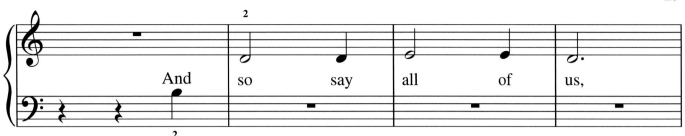

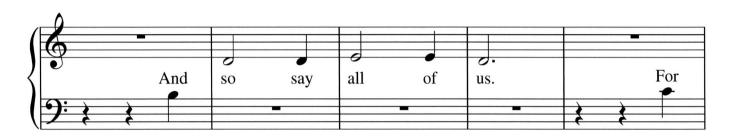

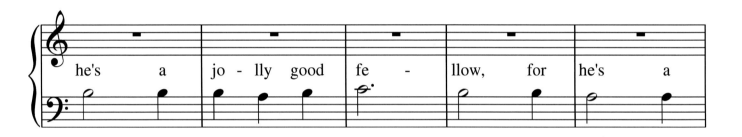

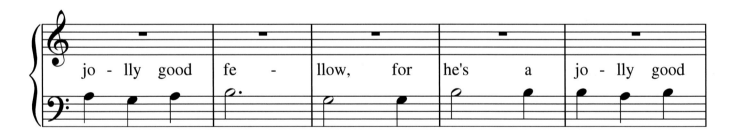

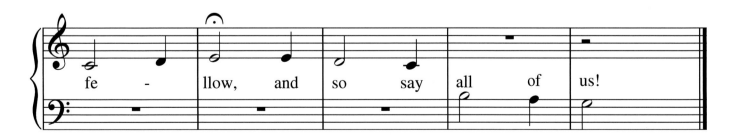

HIP HIP HOORAY!

THE TIE

A tie is when a note is joined, with a curved liine, to another one on the same line or space. It means that the second note isn't played again, but just held on.

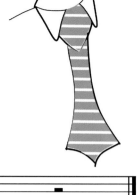

ALL TIED UP

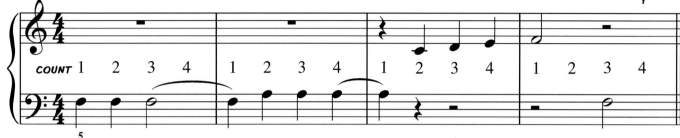

MY HAT IT HAS THREE CORNERS

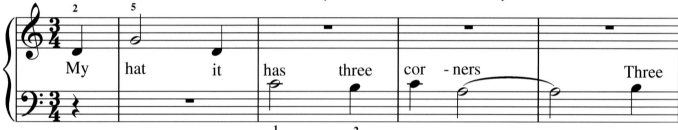

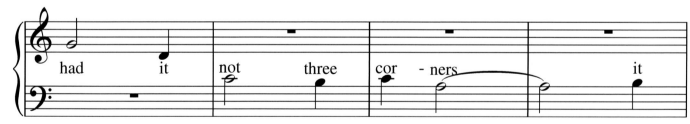

CLAPPING GAME

Clap this rhythm:

Can you tell what this tune is just by clapping it? (Answer on the last page)

If playing Happy Birthday with an accompaniment, play it one octave higher than written.

HAPPY BIRTHDAY TO YOU!

Ha-ppy birth- day to you, ha-ppy birth-day to you. Ha-ppy

birth - day dear_____ Ha-ppy birth-day to you!

Accompaniment for HAPPY BIRTHDAY

PLAYING HANDS TOGETHER

You will be able to play much more interesting music if you can learn to play notes in the left hand and right hand together. It is tricky at first but if you keep practicing you will get the hang of it eventually.

Try this easy exercise to get you started. Here you will be using the same fingers in each hand most of the time.

EXERCISE 1: HANDS TOGETHER - FINGERS 12345

EXERCISE 2: HANDS TOGETHER - TAKE IT SLOW

In the next exercise the hands are doing different things - try it very slowly!

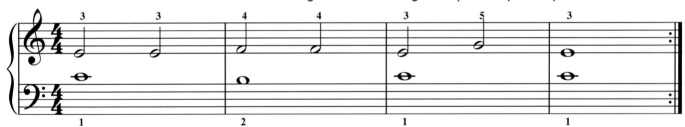

KUM BA YAH

MUSICAL TERMS:
TEMPO

TEMPO
The word tempo means speed. So when we talk of the tempo of a piece of music we are talking about how fast it is.
Three musical words you should remember are:

Lento - which means 'slow'
Andante - which means 'at a medium speed'
Allegro - which means 'quickly'

When you play the next three tunes make sure you remember to play them at the correct tempo.

HURRY, HURRY!

Allegro

TROTTING ALONG

Andante

STEADY NOW - NO RUSH

Lento

TOGETHER AGAIN

Andante

SAY THESE NOTE NAMES

QUICK QUIZ

Find these notes on the piano as quickly as you can:

In the right hand: D F E G C

In the left hand: B C G F A

MUSICAL TERMS:
DYNAMICS

DYNAMICS
When we talk about the dynamics we mean how loud or soft the music is. In printed music you will often see instructions telling you what volume to play. Try to remember what these words mean:

forte – which is shortened to f and means 'loud'
piano – which is shortened to p and means 'quiet'
crescendo – which means gradually getting louder
diminuendo – which means gradually getting quieter

When you play the next two tunes make sure you remember to follow the dynamics AND the tempo directions.

SLOW

Lento

THE TORTOISE

p *cresc.* f

Allegro   ### THE SPRINTER

f

FAST

SAY THESE NOTE NAMES

THE MOCKING BIRD

Andante

p

OLD MACDONALD HAD A FARM

Allegro

Old Mac - don -ald | had a farm. | E - I - E - I

O | And | on that farm he | had a duck. | E - I - E - I - O | With a

quack quack here, | quack, quack there, | here a quack, there a quack,

ev - ry where a quack quack | Old Mac-don -ald | had a farm. | E - I - E - I - O

Accompaniment for Old Macdonald

mp

Staccato

STACCATO
If a note has a dot above or below it you should make that note very short and separate it from the following note.

Your hands should feel very bouncy when you are playing staccato.

37

Andante

FRUIT AND NUTS

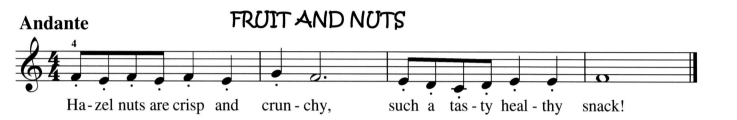

Ha-zel nuts are crisp and crun-chy,   such a tas-ty heal-thy snack!

Lento

THE CLOCK

Tick   tock,   tick   tock,   now   it's   near-ly   bed   time.

Allegro

SOME FOLKS DO

Some folks like to sigh,   some folks do,   some folks do.

Some folks like to sigh,   but   that's   not   me   and   you.

FINGER GYM

When you are learning to play the piano it is important to make sure that you keep your fingers fit and flexible.

The next tune will give your fingers a good workout. Make sure you try to play with a really even tone and at a controlled tempo.

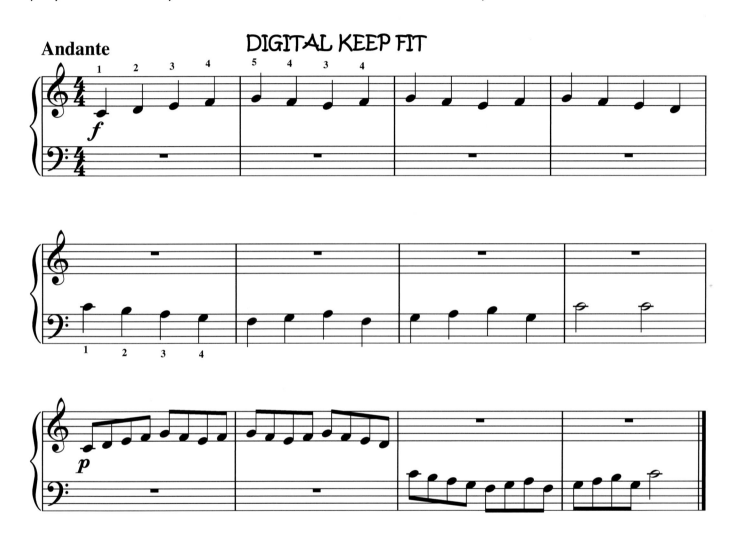

TECHNICAL TIPS

How you hold your fingers on the keys and how you sit are really important:

* Remember, always keep your fingers gently curved
* Keep finger nails trimmed quite short
* Sit up straight

This is an American gospel tune. It should be played quite loud and fast and with a happy smile on your face!

WHEN THE SAINTS GO MARCHING IN!

Answer: the clapping tune on page 31
is AWAY IN A MANGER

This note is the C
which is 8 notes
below middle C

Congratulations!

You have now completed Let's Play Piano Part One

Name...

Date ....

Teacher's Signature....................

More books for young pianists

Young pianists will love these exciting books which have been designed to make practice fun and easy!

PIANO SCALES GRADE 1

It can be difficult to remember all of the notes and fingering for scales, and standard musical notation can be difficult for young pianists.

This book presents every scale as a picture, each showing the fingers which should be used on the keys.

Students will have their scales and broken chords memorized in no time!

PIANO GRADE 1 - in easy steps

Pianists who want to take grade 1 but need to approach it in easy steps can try these pre grade 1 books. They each contain a selection of all of the types of test which are found in a real grade 1 exam:

> 9 pieces, Scales and broken chords
> Aural tests, Theory
> Mark sheet and certificate

MUSIC MANUSCRIPT BOOK

Kids love learning to draw treble and bass clefs and can take their first steps in music composition with this fun little manuscript book.

Six large staves on each page make this super easy for littlies to use.

SMOKE SIGNALS

Get those feet tapping with these rhythmic and tuneful pieces! Each piece comes with a colourful illustration and bite size facts about American Indian history.
The tunes are suitable for ages 7 and up and progress in standard from very easy to about grade 1.

13782268R00026